By the same Author

FUN WITH FLOWERS

PICTURES WITH FLOWERS

MORE PICTURES WITH FLOWERS

101 IDEAS FOR FLOWER ARRANGEMENT

FIRST STEPS WITH FLOWERS

MY ROSES

FLORAL ROUNDABOUT

PARTY PIECES

FUN WITHOUT FLOWERS

by

JULIA CLEMENTS

VAN NOSTRAND · NEW YORK

*Printed in Great Britain for the Publishers
by The Vandyck Printers Ltd., Bristol and London,
bound by A. W. Bain & Co. Ltd., London*

Contents

List of Colour Plates

Foreword

I HAVE always been an optimist, often to my cost; but when, in 1949, Julia Clements suggested that I should publish her first book on flower arranging, so aptly titled FUN WITH FLOWERS, I hesitated. My first reaction was to wonder whether her enthusiasm for the subject was not swamping my sense of publishing realism.

But Julia was unwavering in her belief in the future of flower arranging. She was not to be deterred and she may even have bullied me a little! Finally, I agreed to take the risk and publish a first edition of 5,000 copies. Even then she was not satisfied and so great was her enthusiasm that before going to press I increased the print order, not without some qualms, to 10,000 copies. I was wrong, for in a few months I had to print a further 10,000.

It is now common knowledge that Julia's enthusiasm for her subject has inspired literally hundreds of thousands of others. FUN WITH FLOWERS has been followed by six more books—each with a different and original slant.

Now comes FUN WITHOUT FLOWERS. I wish that I had had some part in the production of this, but my active publishing days are over. When I consider the title and scope of this book I realize that the wheel has come full circle, and I have the greatest pleasure in wishing it the success which I know it deserves, and which I am sure it will achieve.

Good luck, Julia.

THEO A. STEPHENS

Dedicated to all those members of Flower Clubs who have so devotedly spread the love and use of plant material.

Introduction

IN 1949, when my first book FUN WITH FLOWERS was written, post-war restrictions and rationing were still imposed upon us and there seemed little available that could be used to satisfy creative desires. In searching round for something to combat this negative state of affairs it occurred to me that flowers and plants were the only things in which Britain abounded which were not restricted, rationed, or even wanted for export.

The passage between that time and the present is a fascinating story which I hope to tell one day; but most of us now know that Flower Arrangement or the expressive use of flowers and other plant material has been enthusiastically accepted by tens of thousands of men, women and children, who have formed Flower Clubs to further their interest.

In travelling round the country to foster and stimulate this interest it has been my pleasure to visit new housing estates, City Women's Groups, hospitals, schools, hotels—yes, and even prisons!—and I have discovered that despite our wealth of plant material, flowers themselves are not always readily available to everyone. But thousands of enthusiasts in the country have easy access to leaves, berries, root wood, branches and hedgerow wildings, while in cities many buy and carefully tend pot plants, using flowers only on special occasions.

It is as another facet of the art of Flower Arranging that I present this book which, without any hesitation, I entitle FUN WITHOUT FLOWERS, believing that there are just as many thousands who wish to be creative with the grouping of plants, fruits and leaves as there are those who have access to, or can afford to buy, an abundance of flowers.

It brings the creative art ot arranging plant material within the scope of all, for whether you are a bachelor with one branch and a pot plant, a teenager with a collection of shells, or a flat-dweller with only a window-box, you can make the most of what you have as successfully as can the proud possessor of a garden full of flowers or the owner of a large conservatory.

I hope the book will extend the range of thought of the many thousands already dedicated to flower arrangement, and be an incentive to the newcomers to this satisfying and rewarding hobby.

JULIA CLEMENTS

Chelsea, 1961

Fun Without Flowers

YOU may think that enough has already been written on the arrangement of flowers, leaves and plants, and I might once have agreed. But as the years pass I know that this is not true, for as I become more intrigued with the subject so I become more than ever convinced that there is no end to its fascination and importance.

Many others have become similarly enthralled by this easily approachable art, which has led thousands of enthusiasts to the actual growing of plant material; for no arranger exists long without wanting to grow *this* particular interesting leaf or *that* dramatic-looking plant which will give his or her picture just that extra touch of individuality.

In Britain we are particularly lucky, for we are rich in flowers, trees and shrubs, and I am sure that it is this immediate accessibility of growing things that makes it easy for anyone to be an artist with plant material.

When talking to new groups of flower arrangers, I always stress the fact that the subject does not require a lot of study, and appeals to so many because of the rapid results achieved. It was indeed because a picture with flowers and foliage could be made so quickly and look so beautiful that I decided many years ago to go out and try to share my enthusiasm with others.

One of my journeys took me unexpectedly to occupied Western Germany. It appeared that morale was low among the wives of servicemen, and I was asked if I could help them to develop a new interest. I was delighted with the prospect of such a journey and felt sure that I could fire them with my own enthusiasm for flower arrangement; but on my arrival I found to my surprise that no flowers were available. I spoke at sixteen different stations, each in the heart of the country and miles from ordinary shops, and at each I was met with the cry that it was hopeless to start because they had no flowers. Not to be daunted—and I love a challenge—I would look out of the window at the surrounding country and say "But you have paradise. Surely with pine cones, the wood, the moss, the stones, leaves and branches, even with the fruit on the table, we can have great fun *without* flowers."

And when the tour was over I realised that I had never had such fun before. It was also rewarding, for later I heard that these Service exiles had started to explore the countryside, making interpretive plant designs and challenging one another's stations to arrangement competitions.

I have had similar experiences when speaking in convalescent hospitals, where I have been overjoyed when watching the faces of patients discovering for the first time the wonder of plants. Once they have been shown how, they quickly become adept at searching for the items and then grouping them according to their individual taste; and although I needed no proof I have letters which convince me that the creative use of plant material can act as a therapy to many with long illnesses, to convalescents, or to any of us who feel bored or unhappy or just in a rut.

It would be foolish to deny that the addition of flowers to any decoration makes the result more lovely, but my purpose in this book is to help the many arrangers who find themselves without flowers. Townswomen are apt to think, misguidedly, that all countrywomen are lucky because they have an abundance of flowers, but this is not always the case. Though many countrywomen do manage to keep their gardens colourful and gay, not all grow enough flowers for constant picking. Nor does the country exactly abound in flower shops. But leaves, branches, nuts, cones, ferns, twigs, bracken, berries and so many other wild plant items are plentiful—and free!

If we keep our eyes open for suitable material and use a little imagination, we can all make living plant pictures. It is just a question of placing various sizes, shapes and colours together in such a way that each shows off the other to the best advantage, and it is not really difficult, as you will see from the arrangements in the following pages, which I very much hope will stimulate your own ideas. It is too easy always to do the same things, so try something different; you and your friends will be delighted with the result.

Once you feel the pleasure of creating an arrangement you will quickly develop a more "seeing eye" and will be better able to assess the value of the items around you. I remember an October visit to one of my favourite hotels, set on a cliff top in southern England and amid pine trees, heather, bracken and other bush growth. I was greeted on arrival by a request from the owner's wife that I should not look too closely at her flower decorations, which she said had suffered from the seasonal expensiveness of flowers and the time stolen from her busy life by their purchase and arrangement. I smiled and wondered if I dared suggest something I had often thought, which was that she should use some of the interesting plant material that was in the grounds, making it not into formal placements but into interesting interpretive pieces illustrative of the district. I explained that the many visitors coming from London who were so accustomed to seeing the accepted bowl of flowers would be really thrilled to be greeted by decorations typical of the surroundings.

To illustrate my point I later made a design for the reception desk. Finding a most interesting piece of weathered wood under a tree, I pressed it firmly into a wodge of Plasticine which held it firmly in the base of a green earthenware oven-dish. (A tray or any other shallow receptacle could have been used.) I filled the dish with sand, soil and moss; then I placed pieces of rock around the wood, and in between them I inserted groups of dried heather (the flowering season was over) and small ferns. Behind the wood were placed some sprays of pine, and a few cones were grouped low down. It took very little time to make, and with water added to the dish it proved to be very long-lasting and required no attention. She was delighted and the next day almost ran into the grounds to pick masses of rhododendron leaves, broom, more heather, pine cones and other items. With these she made arrangements for other parts of the hotel, which were more suitable to the background and surroundings and gave a lot of pleasure to her visitors.

So even if you are without flowers, do open your eyes to what is near at hand, be it fruit, leaves, shells, wood, cones, or any of the hundreds of items that can be made into interesting compositions.

Have you noticed at flower shows how often there has been a class for "All Green", or "Foliage Only" or "Flowerless Beauty"? These have drawn the greatest number of entries, the exhibitors creating the most interesting and beautiful arrangements; and in fact you have only to visit any of the thousands of flower shows and floral art exhibitions that are staged all over the country each year to realise what a wonderful means of expression the use of plant material has proved to all those who enter.

So if you want to be an artist without flowers do not be afraid to make a start. Never be intimidated by wondering what others might think. Be yourself: make a grouping now and allow your picture to be your very own. Whether you place a bare branch in a bowl, adding some rhododendron leaves low down and stabilising the whole with a few stones, or insert a few sprays of golden privet behind a piece of rock in a pottery dish, it is *your* creation and until you wish to learn more, or try something different, your first picture should give you tremendous satisfaction.

In the beginning, however, I advise you not to pay too much attention to principles, for although a knowledge of them will finally take you further along the road to success, they really belong to the middle of your study. At first you need to *do* something, anything, as long as you start.

Later on, if you wish to become a really expressive arranger, comes the study of design, composition, rhythmic movement, transition, repetition, textures, colours and forms. This period, while meant as a time of improvement, often holds the arranger back, for she is more concerned with technicalities than with the development of her own ideas. Later, when these technicalities have become second nature to her, she will find herself able to branch out on her own, and to reject this cramping adherence to principles. They are still there of course, but they are now so automatic that although the artist is constantly guided by them, she works without being aware of them. So let us look at them as they apply to plant arrangements.

Design

No grouping of any items can appear integrated or attractive without a feeling for design. Study the following symbols and you will see what I mean.

|||| — . . S S . . || —

 |
|.|
— · S S · —
|·|
 |

As they appear first they are just lines and dots, but when re-grouped in accordance with principles of design they make an acceptable pattern. So it is with plants, leaves and fruit. By placing the tallest and slenderest material, whether it be tall wood or fine green sprays, on the outside, and the bigger, more dominant items at the focus of attention at the base of the main stems, the eye is led from the outside or top of the design to the hub of interest, where the eye should rest. Design means the joining together of items of different size, form and colour into a unified whole, this co-ordination of stems or items being emphasized by dominant interest.

In foliage arrangements dominant interest could be a group of variegated leaves; with fruit it could be the brightest or most shiny piece, and in plant arrangements it could be the largest-leaved plant. Large stones and chunks of wood can also be items of dominant interest. The spot in the design where the dominant interest is placed is often termed the focal point, the heart or the hub of the design.

Transition

Items used in transition are those which take the eye from, for example, fine sprays to broad leaf. They should soften the move from one item to another, and are placed between contrasts. Imagine a painting in which a narrow path leads you to a red-roofed white cottage: here the cottage is the dominant interest or focal point, the path being the titivating touch which leads you from the outside of the picture to the heart of it. Yet the artist will have placed along the path a shrub or a puddle, or a twist—any subtle move that will break up the suddenness of the thin path to the solid cottage. So, when composing with plant material, you need some "in between" items as transition. They should not be as strong as the strongest or as noticeable as the highlights. They could be grey leaves to soften two strong colours, or an insignificant item to act as a buffer between two equally good items. You may be using bright fruit grouped at the base of drift-wood, in which case a trail of mellowing vine leaves with ends twined about the fruit will soften the junction.

Transition is a principle which is not always practised within the arrangement, but it is important to understand it. For instance on the narrow window-sill of my London flat I have a four-footed gilt jardinière which contains three nephrolepsis ferns side by side. Anyone seeing this small grouping might rightly argue that I have not practised the principle of transition, since the ferns are all of the same texture and size. Superficially this is quite true; but if the eye wanders further it will be noticed that the ferns are acting as a transition across the inverted shape of the net curtain opening, the jardinière, which is bright and solid, being the focal point. In other words any arrangement is only part of the whole setting; and in this particular case the narrow shelf would not take a wider container with a placement of different sized plants. It is knowing how to break the rules that is important, and this only comes with practice.

Scale

Scale means proportion. To scale one's decoration to fit the background in which it will be seen is to keep it in proportion with the other items in the room. It means also keeping the plant material in proportion with the container used, as well as scaling the plant items with each other. For instance, fine ferns or carrot leaves, although most decorative, would not appear happy placed with large broad funkia leaves, neither would the fine leaves be ideally suited to a pottery container. Yet these same leaves would combine well with plantain seed spikes in a glass container. A tall rubber plant (*Ficus elastica*), if you like it, will decorate a corner in a lofty room, whereas a grouping of *Begonia rex* leaves backed perhaps with a tall vine or Sansevieria would complement a setting in a lower ceilinged, panelled room. Many a delicate drawing-room might be enhanced with trails of ivy, ruffled ferns or tradescantia. So I advise you to think of your setting when planning your plants, and choose them in accordance with the background against which they will be seen.

Textures

Textures are important. A couturier will place a touch of silk or velvet against a dull surface to emphasize a particular line or aspect of his creation; and the plant arranger searches likewise for the contrasting textures that will produce most effect. A shiny leaf will add brilliance to a grouping of dull surfaced leaves, just as the varnish-like finish of green peppers will highlight a grouping of such duller-surfaced fruits and vegetables as pears, artichokes, cucumbers and egg plants with Swiss chard leaves. Certain leaves, such as heavier *Begonia rex* and paeony, will supply depth and main interest in a design; while the finer trails, like ivy, rosemary, or artemisia are more suitable for the outside of the arrangement. I often place the large swerving leaves of the onopordon thistle on the outside of a large pedestal group, and in this you may argue that I am contradicting myself, for surely the flat surface of these large leaves should not be used as framework or outside material. I should explain that as these leaves are grey, they are therefore visually light; they are also long, pointed and swerving and are in good scale for a large group. This means that if they are used on the outside, something much bolder and more dominant, such as artichoke heads, onion seedheads or their own thistle heads should be used in the centre. Of course it would look wrong if, after making the framework with these leaves, the centre were finished with delicate leaves or grasses, because the weight would then be in the wrong place. So do open your eyes to the textural value of different leaves and plants.

Colour

You may think that a reference to colour is out of place in a book that does not mention flowers. I do not agree, because there is a considerable range of colour in leaves alone that can be exploited to good effect. Foliage is by no means all monotone, for there are nearly as many highlights among the tints of leaves as there are in flowers. For years I have been studying colour and its qualities, but I do not think it should be over-emphasized to the uninitiated flower arranger. Such casual advice as "by mixing a little white with a colour a tint can be obtained" can be very confusing, for we must remember that as artists with living plant material we are using nature's gifts and not paints, and nothing we, as arrangers, can do will alter the colour of the plants we group together. What is important is to know *where* to place plants of certain colours for best effect either in a design or in a room.

However, before we can talk about colour we must agree on terminology. A TINT is a lighter version of a colour (i.e. lime and apple green are *tints* of green) and tints are generally better used as highlights. They may be introduced in the centre of a design as focal interest, or if used on their own may become the highlight of a dark corner in a room. Similarly a SHADE is a darker version of a colour, so that bottle green is a *shade* of green, and is better used to bring a number of light elements in a room together, or to give depth to a plant or leaf arrangement.

Red-shaded leaves, such as *Prunus pissardii*, rhus, maple, and beetroot are useful, although if massed they will appear dull in an arrangement unless given light with a few tinted leaves, berries or seedheads. When making an autumn foliage and berry decoration not long ago, I used tall pale green iris seedheads for height with sprays of copper beech as framework. To change the form rusty green seedheads were worked in nearer the centre, which was filled with the maroon-coloured penny shaped leaves of rhus (*Cotinus coggygria*). This shade in the centre might have appeared as a hole when seen from a distance, so a grouping of pale green crab apples was inserted. Pale grasses were used as highlights to break up the nearness of the paeony and rhus leaves, and the design appeared just as full of life and colour as if the vase had been filled with the flowers of high summer.

I generally find it better not to distribute my colours evenly, so when faced with a choice I suggest that you either make your design predominantly shaded, introducing a few tints, or use mainly tints, focalising with shades. Obviously there will be variations between these extremes, but in the main it is better to allow one to be subordinate to the other.

Composition

Every flower, leaf or plant arrangement is in itself a composition, although in show schedules this word is generally taken to include accessories. Here I will discuss composition with particular reference to non-floral arrangement, because so many novices wonder how to begin. The secret of composing is to bring together a number of elements in a rhythmic movement that finishes on a pleasing note: so when setting out to make a composition collect all your items and decide which of them shall be used for main interest, because everything you want to express with them cannot be of equal importance. If therefore you have picked onion seedheads and artichoke heads for the centre, it would be better to eliminate one of them, just as you must decide between bright green peppers and pale yellow lemons for main interest in a grouping of fruit, because the rest of the composition must be subordinate to one dominant interest only.

Of course this will be much simpler if you can decide what you want before picking or buying. Suppose that when looking for leaves in the garden you find some flushed green megasea leaves which you think will be ideal for central interest: you will then look for some different shapes to go behind them, finally searching for fine sprays for the outside. In a smaller garden you might find a twisted branch to give height to a modern design, and use the megasea leaves for transition to your main interest, which could be apples, cones, or a piece of tree wood. So you will find composition easier if you look for

1. Tall fine outside material.
2. Medium interest transition material.
3. More interesting main items that are dominant in shape or colour.

The best plant arrangers study these principles until they are instinctive and once they require no effort to bring them to mind they can visualise a grouping round any living plant form almost at once. With plants in particular they will automatically "see" that the tall one should be at the back, placing the trailing one at the side, with the broad-leafed one at the base of the tall one. It is this quick assessment of different forms, shapes and colours that simplifies the grouping of living plant material.

Make your own containers

One of the extra fascinations of composing with plant material is the search for unusual containers. As much study should be given to the selection of containers as to the choice of plants, for they are part of the picture and can have as much interest of colour, texture, form and scale as the plants themselves. Containers can be delicate or coarse—glass or silver for maidenhair ferns, and pottery or wood for heavy leaves and seedheads. Baskets make ideal containers for a mixed group of plants, while copper, brass and pewter are often the best choice for leaves and plants of similar colourings. A plant of grey *Stachys lanata* transferred to a pewter mug can make an inexpensive and appealing decoration on a writing desk. Again, a ravishing and long-lasting effect may be had with a plant of *Grevillia robusta* placed in a copper or brass container. If the plant is left out of doors to harden it a little the lower leaves will turn to a shade of burnished gold.

Most of us have a number of what might be termed "old-fashioned" flower vases, which make excellent plant containers. For years I kept one such opaque glass vase at the back of a cupboard, thinking that its tall, epergne-like shape was old-fashioned. Then one day I dropped a pot containing a chlorophytum plant and not having another handy I wrapped the roots and a little soil in a polythene bag and inserted this in the fluted top of the glass vase. It looked quite lovely, the swerved, grass-like leaves spreading out and down over the sides of the narrow stemmed vase. This led me to use a number of "accepted" flower vases for my plants, some of which are illustrated on pages 53 and 55.

Shells make interesting containers for growing plants or cut foliage, and their attractive insides may often be left uncovered. An empty shell backed with sea-fern and grasses can dominate an arrangement; and if you place sprays of grey artemisia or pink Rose Bay willow herb gone to seed on a pin-holder in the base of an up-turned clam shell they can give the impression of plumes waving in the sea. Placing the shell on a black wooden base or small tray protects the furniture and adds to the picture. The large pale green snail shells, irridescent on the outside and pearly inside, are so jewel-like on their own that I hesitate to place anything in the opening but a few tall, fine green sprays. These leaves not only give height but draw attention to the beauty of the shell.

Small shells of any kind, thrown around the base of a pin-holder in a shallow dish of water, make interesting under-water decorations.

Common scallop shells are not to be shunned either, for they make delightful individual place setting arrangements, or may be grouped together as a table centrepiece. To do this, make a pile of thick plaster filler powder on a base, inserting perhaps five scallop shells in a circle low down, then three slightly higher at intervals rather like the petals of a flower, finishing with one at the top. I have done this with great success, filling each shell with a small sedum or echeveria plant.

Baskets of all kinds have many uses for plant arrangers. The half-moon shaped shopping baskets that have been in vogue make ideal containers for plants when hung from wall or door, especially if a trailing ivy or tradescantia is added to the grouping. By lining them with a waterproof tin or dish, old fishing creels, basket handbags, hamper baskets, basketware trays, even waste paper baskets become effective containers for fruit and leaves, particularly in a rustic setting: even a summer straw hat or holiday coolie hat upturned and set on a table will provide a good base for a plant or leaf grouping. In fact there are endless potentialities for any form of straw, rush or basket weave in this kind of arrangement.

While thinking of odd items I must mention the fascination bottles have for me. I cannot bear to throw them away because they are so often unexpectedly useful. Stone cider and pickling jars combine well with fruit, wheat and berries for autumn arrangements and have a tremendous appeal when placed on old oak dressers or other country backgrounds.

Nothing is quite such fun as making your own containers. Although I am a very busy person I become as excited as a child when buying a small bag of cement and dashing home to mix it. I mix the cement with either clear varnish or flat or glossy paint, using any colour that is desired : I find that a dull brown gives a useful rough wood effect. The mixture is then spread on the outside of tins and the paint or varnish helps it to adhere to the smooth surface. To vary the surface texture imprints of buttons, etc., can be made, and the appearance of ridged wood may be achieved by stroking the outside with a fork before the cement sets. Pastel coloured effects can be obtained by covering tins with a mixture of Polyfilla, the white plaster powder, to which a dye or a few spots of coloured ink may be added to give the desired effect. Writing of pastel colours reminds me of the time I painted a tin colander with mauve paint, planting it later with pink and purple petunias, and hanging it, with great effect, over the door of my studio. Think of the variations of colour that could be used with such a painted item, which could stand or be hung, like mine, from a coloured cord.

Another idea is to get a piece of wood about 18″ × 12″ from the local carpenter and, about 2″ in from all corners, fix cotton reels to act as feet. Then, to one side or on the centre of this little table screw an empty tin, either a baking tin or a pie dish. Finally, to ensure that the whole is watertight insert a second tin inside the first one. Then paint it all black. This makes an original container, and of course it could be painted in other colours. If you first coat the tin with vinegar and allow it to dry the paint will adhere much more readily.

Here is another novel suggestion: screw a cork to the centre of the underside of a tin pie dish, drop candle-grease or sealing-wax round the cork to prevent any leakage of water, and insert the cork into a decorative wine bottle. The bottle should be weighted first by filling it with water (plain if the glass is coloured, and vice versa), and the result will be a most attractive container for short-stemmed flowers with drooping foliage.

Arrangements with ***Wood***

Arrangements With Wood

WOOD in all its fascinating shapes and forms can be an inspiration to the flower arranger. It can be a straight, seasoned slab of wood smoothed by the carpenter and used as a base, or a slice of tree wood untouched except by the saw. It can be a twisted branch, or an eerie wisp of a dead root that will eventually give height to an otherwise low design of plants, or a piece of drift wood which in turn has been sculptured by the winds, sea and rain. We in Britain have only recently become aware of the beauty of weathered wood but, as eyes are opened to the value of these attractive forms, more and more designers are using it, sometimes for height, but often as a dominant note in a design featuring a few flowers or leaves.

I love the natural colour of wood, especially those pieces that have become greyed and hardened by the elements. At other times ivy roots, peeled of their bark and left shiny white, please me because their pale colouring gives a light touch to dark green leaves. Dark burls of oak are excellent when set against the light grey-green of echeverias or sedums, while burnt and blackened gorse wood will give strong line and emphasis to any lighter-coloured ferns or leaves that might form part of a design. Ordinary slices of tree wood can be rubbed with a cloth dipped in linseed oil and powdered pumice-stone. This smooths and polishes and preserves the wood. Pale woods can be stained and polished with darker shoe polish, rough edges can be sand-papered and coaxed into required shapes, whilst it is easy to fix two or more pieces together with screws or nails in order to obtain a firm wooden set piece which can dramatise your plant arrangements.

Try using wood and discover its beauty yourself.

This design combines wood, fixed to a base in a large pottery bowl, with three living plants, all in their pots. The tallest fern is placed at the back, the echeveria and the smaller fern in front. Moss, stones and wood hide the pots.

A piece of manzanita wood gives height to this arrangement. Pressed into Plasticine and backed with stones, the wood is held firm, and the dish is filled with gravel, sand, soil and charcoal. Glacier ivy and small rosettes of Sempervivum montanum *grow from between wood and stones, a pteris fern is set at the left, and the surface covered with moss.*

Another design featuring growing plants — pots of grape ivy and maranta stand behind an interestingly-shaped piece of oak, held by Plasticine in a large pottery dish. The plants can be watered in situ.

EFFECTIVE USE OF
STRIPPED IVY ROOT

Step 1:
The ivy root is placed in position and a pot of glacier ivy set behind the wood.

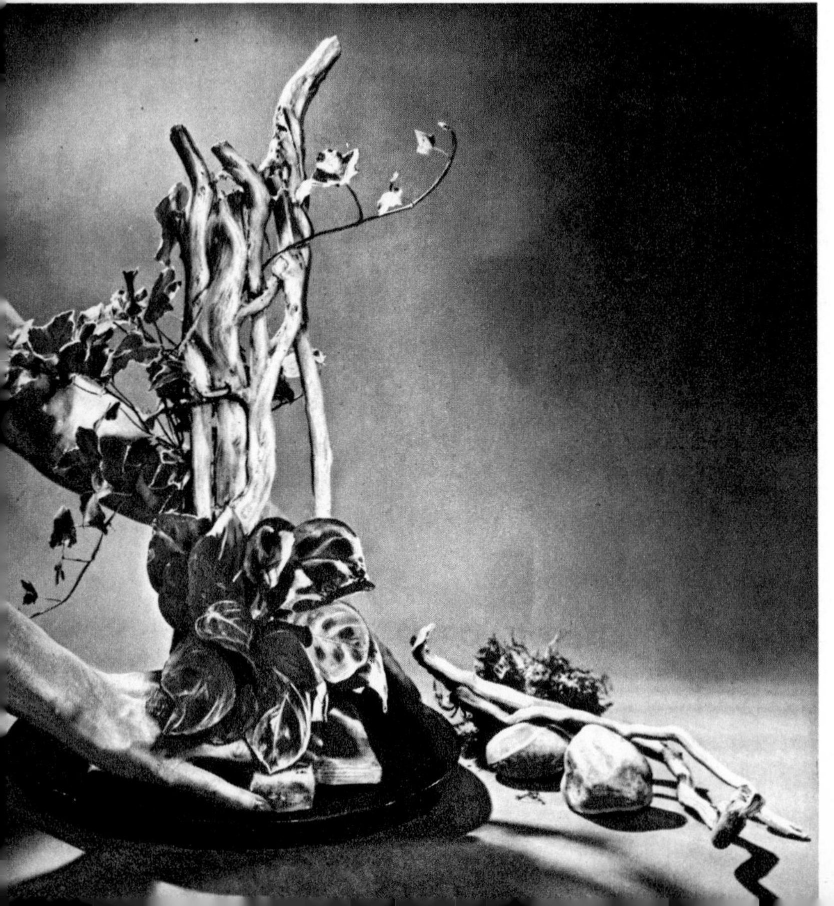

Step 2:
The pot of maranta is tilted forward in front . . .

Step 3: (*opposite*)
. . . and the pots are hidden with stones and moss and more wood. Watering can be done without disturbing the arrangement.

Step 3: (*opposite*)
The design is finished by the insertion of stems of pale green Jacob's ladder, behind and in front of the wood. The white and pale green colouring was most effective against the terra-cotta of the pottery.

LARGE DESIGN
SUITABLE FOR HALL

Step 1: (*above*)
A twisted piece of ivy root is placed on the rim of the container, which has a dish of water inside.

Step 2:
Three fatsia leaves are added at different angles to give a three-dimensional effect.

SAND, STONES AND SEDUM

Step 1:
A heap of sand and moss is made in a shallow dish, onto which a piece of wood is placed.

Step 2:
A pot of Sedum sieboldii *is placed behind the wood, and a cut rosette of echeveria in the centre.*

Step 3:
More sand and stones are added and another cut echeveria tilted forward at the left. Echeverias last for weeks when cut and tucked into sand. They may even take root.

Wood, leaves and fruit make this colourful decoration. Megasea leaves are held in a small dish of water placed behind the twisted ivy root. Lemons add a dominant note to an unusual design.

Arrangements with ***Fruit***

Arrangements With Fruit

FRUIT with its infinite variety of shape, colour and texture offers some of the most fascinating material for the arranger to work with. There is never a time of the year when some kind of fruit is not available and, if cleverly placed in juxtaposition with leaves, branches or drift wood it can help to make most original decorations for the home or show.

There need be little waste attached to a fruit arrangement, for it can always be eaten when one is tired of the design; and when flowers are scarce it provides the best answer to the constant cry of "How shall I decorate the dining table?"

Although it seems easier to resort to using mixed fruit, do try an all-green arrangement using green apples, green grapes and dull green avocado pears with shiny green leaves. This would be most effective, especially if other colours are contained on the chinaware. Imagine, too, the cool beauty of a pyramid arrangement of lemons, flanked each side by lemon-coloured candles, the candlesticks surrounded low down with green leaves.

Some fruits are shiny, some have dull surfaces, some grow singly, others in bunches. Try placing the different forms, sizes and shapes in such positions that they form a pattern or design. Half fill a bowl with tissue paper or wire, then pile the fruit on top of it; on a platter set some of the lower fruit on rubber jar rings to avoid them slipping about and join other items together with the aid of toothpicks. Arranging fruit can be fun!

Frosted grapes, arranged on tiers of white china cake-stands, make an attractive decoration for the table or sideboard. A small vase holds the bow of pink ribbon at the top, and extra bows are tucked into each tier.

The well-defined, ribbed hosta lily leaves are not only long-lasting, but give excellent contrast of form to the fine sprays of oats in this arrangement on a wooden base. They are held on a pin-holder in a dish of water, hidden by root-wood and bunches of grapes.

A framed wall mirror made an ideal base for this grouping of fruit suitable for a side or buffet table. The candlesticks were placed first to give height to the design.

An interesting decoration for a Harvest Festival celebration. The hand sickle is fixed into a small jar made firm on the base with Plasticine. The jar also holds stems of long-eared wheat, while the leaves are placed in a jar of water behind the sickle. The items of fruit are held in position by toothpicks.

Fatsia japonica *leaves make a dramatic foil for the mixed colourings and shapes of the fruit heaped in this large pottery bowl. The leaves are held in a dish of water hidden by the fruit.*

(opposite)
Suitable for a small dinner table, an ornate gilded jardinière holds pale green grapes and peaches. The lime-green candle is fixed to its base by a ring of Plasticine (see page 117).

An attractive design for a sideboard uses sprays of ivy, rhododendron and variegated privet held in water behind a large piece of tree wood. Green grapes continue the line of the design, while two deeper green wine bottles complete the effect.

The colourful heap of fruit in this decoration for a side-table is shown off to great advantage against the silver grey of the pewter plate and tankard.

FRUIT FOR
INFORMAL OCCASIONS

Step 1:
Because of its size and colouring, the stew-pot, held on a knob of Plasticine, is placed at the right for dominant interest. Behind it tall stems of dried maize flowers are fixed on a pin-holder in a dish of water.

Step 2:
Grapes are added flowing out of the stew-pot for central interest, apples prepared with toothpicks are made ready and vine leaves are placed at the back.

Step 3: (*opposite*)
Second thoughts about the position of the smaller stew-pots! And the tray is now completely covered with a variety of fruit. Leaves are tucked in water.

Pale green apples combine well with the light brown colouring of an interesting piece of oak wood. Fixed on a pin-holder in a dish behind the wood are three stems of golden privet and, to give contrast of form, two sprays of magnolia.

Arrangements with *Plants*

Arrangements With Plants

THE day has gone when single plants were placed in china or plastic pots and left to stand in isolated glory. Today the grouping of plants as a decoration appeals to every arranger both for the satisfaction it gives and for the beauty of the collective effect.

Three plants of the same variety set in a row have not the same decorative appeal as three of different kinds; and when choosing plants for an arrangement look for height, depth and focal interest.

Plants such as sansevieria, grevillia and croton are excellent for establishing height in a grouping, while the large-leafed *Begonia rex*, dieffenbachia and ficus will give depth. Smaller plants with variegated colourings such as *Peperomia maranta* and chlorophytum will add focal interest and any trailing plants such as ivy and tradescantia are excellent for side placements and to swerve down over the container.

One of the joys of plant arrangements is that they do not demand unending attention. I find the attraction in making these groupings is in testing one's ability to combine certain shapes and colours in the vast variety of containers that can be brought into use.

Old mahogany tea caddies or work-boxes look most effective when filled with plants, as do old-fashioned corner wash-stands and bric-à-brac brackets. Tankards, vegetable dishes, apothecaries' jars and wine bottles make excellent plant containers, while many of the modern vases, difficult for flowers, assume an importance of their own when filled with a single plant.

A lovely grouping of five pot plants in a large stoneware drip pan, placed around piece of root wood held firm by Plasticine. The tall grevillea is at the back, to give height; the maranta, for spotted interest, low down. Ivy and tradescantia flow out over the brim.

A lime-green straw basket makes an interesting container for pots of green and white chlorophytum and pale green tradescantia. If stood on saucers the plants can be watered where they grow.

A plant pot of ivy assumes a different air when placed in a white and gold china vase. A change of texture is obtained by the addition of white ivy root-wood, held in position by a white stone.

(Opposite)
Tall iris leaves rise from a large black pottery vase, while two plants in pots rest inside the wide opening. The broad leaves of dieffenbachia give interest at the left; the striped chlorophytum leaves trail over the rim. A piece of root-wood hides the pots.

Chlorophytum again, in a white china vase. A piece of twisted root-wood gives rhythmic movement to an otherwise symmetrical design.

Containers play an important part in decorations with plants, for they can add texture and colour to the completed design. This Victorian mahogany tea caddy, the lid lined with green velvet, holds three pot plants — Grevillea robusta *for height, tradescantia for variegated interest, ivy to trail over the edge of the caddy. Visual weight is given by stems of hydrangea leaves in a bottle, inserted at the side.*

Fatsia, canariensis ivy and tradescantia in pots are grouped together to ***make*** *a side table decoration. White finger coral is inserted for extra interest.*

A small plant of silver and maroon Begonia rex, *tilting forward in a stemmed black container, has an airy background of maroon-coloured nigella seedheads. The stems of these are inserted in Plasticine and pressed down on the pot, and the wide top of the container is filled in with moss.*

The perfect thing for a man's desk. The lichen-covered branch is inserted into the pewter tankard and held firm on a pin-holder; then the Asplenium nidus (*bird's nest fern*) *is planted in gravel, sand, charcoal and soil, and the tankard stood on a pewter plate. Nidus grows well indoors, but occasionally needs a little fresh air.*

A tin-lined basket is perhaps the ideal container for a group of growing plants. Here the tall sansevieria gives height at the left back; a lovely glossy spathiphyllum is set in front. Variegated ivy (Hedera canariensis) *makes a highlight in the centre and a smaller indoor ivy trails out at the right. All these plants are easy to grow indoors.*

Philodendron scandens *is one of the easiest of indoor plants to handle, and it likes shade. Here it is trained to a stick and, complete with pot, placed in a white vase to make a decoration for a narrow hall.*

A Denby-ware casserole dish on its stand seems exactly the right container for these two plants. At the left a pot of Rhoicissus rhomboidea *(grape ivy) gives height, and the silver-green tradescantia weaves its way about the piece of pale brown manzanita wood which hides the pots.*

An interesting composition for a modern setting — three pot plants grouped behind a gnarled piece of drift-wood. Height is given by the tall sansevieria, the tri-colour of the dieffenbachia plant adds side interest, while the small, pale green nidus fern makes an excellent foil swerving over the cinnamon brown of the wood.

A piece of rough stone (which could be moulded from sand, cement and straw) makes a home for a Sedum sieboldii *plant. A pot of chlorophytum placed at the back and a delicate white figurine complete a charming design, made on a polished black base.*

Keep a good look-out for out-of-the-ordinary containers, because there will always come a time when they are just what you need for a particular plant or flower. This Victorian copper tea-kettle, for instance, shows up to perfection the delicate silver green tradescantia set in its opening.

An interesting picture made in a wide black pottery bowl held on a tripod. Fatshedera lizei *at the back gives height, while the* Begonia rex *placed centrally gives contrast of foliage form. Ivy and Virginia creeper flow down at the sides and pots of chlorophytum and fern are tilted forward over the rim of the bowl. Shorter, unseen plants are set at the back and all are covered with moss.*

For a low table or a fireplace a brass coal-scuttle makes an attractive container for plants. Here the tallest phoenix fern is placed at the right, with fatsia and the shorter split philodendron lower down. As a change of form and to lighten the effect, chlorophytum is added at the left. Stand the pots on crumpled newspaper, and water them in place.

Arrangements with
Shells and Ornaments

Arrangements With Shells and Ornaments

NEARLY all shells can be used as containers after being made watertight by painting the inside with several coats of varnish or candle wax. Left half exposed, the opening holding tiny sedums or a small succulent, the shape of a shell gives a good outline to many decorations. But it is not always as containers that I visualise the beauty of shells. Standing empty at the base of branches, leaves or plants, with the mysterious interior exposed, they make fascinating points of interest in a design. They can add texture and colour to an arrangement of leaves, just as an interesting ornament will help to tell the story of a composition.

Though some purists object to the use of ornaments with plant material, I myself enjoy their association in house decorations, provided the items are chosen with taste and used in the spirit of the design. Colour and texture should be studied, so that the ornament combines well with the plants or leaves with which it is used. One would not, for instance, surround a wooden elephant with sweetheart roses; nor would a delicate china model of a ballerina be happily placed with large ficus leaves. But the model of a heron, set in a "pool" of water at the side of which is a grouping of leaves and reeds, or a china cockerel dominating an arrangement of corncobs, wheat and fruit, would be entirely appropriate. The ornament must be part of the original scheme, not just added as an afterthought.

Dried grasses and sea-fern give height to this design on a slab of wood. A succulent, Pachyphytum opalescens, *is tilted in its pot for low interest, and moss and shells hide the pot.*

(opposite)
A sea fantasy built up on a brown wooden base. The spider shell contains a starfish-like Cryptanthus zonatus *planted in a little peaty soil, and behind the shell stands a grouping of bulrushes, fern and ivy.*

An unusual container made from two clam shells joined by plaster-cement. The delicate maidenhair fern and broader-leaved peperomia are placed in a mixture of sand, stones and charcoal.

Another arrangement using dried sea fern, held on a pin-holder in a shallow dish. Three echeveria plants live happily tucked into the sand; shells and a pottery fish complete a delightful "seascape".

Three wisps of grevillea foliage, held in a pink pearly shell, sway as though under water. With a few smaller shells and some fish net, and placed against an uncluttered background, this is a simple but most effective decoration.

Grevillea foliage bought from the florist often assumes the feather-like swerve of a parrot's comb. Here three stems are placed in a dish of water behind a white Crown Stafford china parrot, standing on a white latticed tray. Mahonia leaves are added low down, and a few mandarin oranges heighten the colour scheme.

In this design inspired by the Royal Doulton china model "Top o' the Hill" the wind seems to have swept the broom and pussy willow into a curve to complement the swirling skirts of the figurine. Plant material is held on a pin-holder in a small dish of water, covered with stones and moss.

The pottery cockerel takes pride of place at the base of the tall stems of oats in this autumn arrangement using corn cobs, Fatsia japonica *leaves, beans and radishes.*

(opposite)
On a polished black base: one twisted sprig of hawthorn newly in leaf, held on a pin-holder in a dish of water behind a china figurine — simplicity itself, but how effective!

Ornaments can often help tell the story, provided they associate well with the plant material used. This china doe appears to be searching for water at the base of a "tree" held on a pin-holder; grasses, ferns and moss complete the scene.

Arrangements with

Leaves

Arrangements With Leaves

DURING their cycle of life leaves pass through so many interesting phases in size, colour and texture that it is no wonder arrangers are turning more and more to foliage when planning their designs. Even in its dried form it is both useful and appealing. Flower Club members were among the first to show the real beauty of leaves when composed into artistic designs, and often the "Foliage Only" Class at Shows draws the largest number of entries.

Making a pleasing picture with foliage needs an appreciation of texture and shape. There are fine spiky leaves such as iris, gladioli, or sprays of berberis and rosemary—all so good for the main lines of a design; while for central depth or interest there are larger leaves like funkia (hosta), megasea, kale or the grey *Verbascum broussa.* These in their turn contrast with the fine lacy leaves such as *Grevillia robusta,* carrot or the grey centaurea, more suitable for dainty table decorations.

The art is in placing one texture or colour against the other; just as an artist will add a flick of white paint as a highlight and insert a dark patch for depth, so will the practiced flower arranger add a leafy spike or pale grass for highlight, placing darker or flatter leaves for depth. Variegated leaves, such as geranium, canariensis ivy or the hardy hedera, can be placed centrally for focal interest. A mixture of greys and lime green focalised with a touch of maroon can appear as colourful as a mass of flowers—and often more restful and cool-looking.

People living in towns may not always find it easy to obtain a variety of leaves, but a simple arrangement of ivy in a shallow dish, held down by stone chips or chunks of glass, is within the reach of all. Or try tying a few large leaves together and anchor them at the base of a fish tank, hiding the stem ends with coloured marbles. The glistening bubble effect on the edges of the leaves under water is fascinating to watch.

Foliage transpires very freely, so keep your arrangements away from strong draughts or direct sunlight.

Contrast of colour and form are evident in this arrangement of fine grey Artemisia ludoviciana, *branch wood, and low down a few sprays of rhododendron leaves.*

(*opposite*)
An air of coolness is given by this mixture of grey and green leaves in a white vase. Iris leaves and whitebeam give height, fennel and grey artichoke leaves flow out at the sides, Senecio greyi *is placed low in front, with onopordon thistle leaves at the back.*

This delicate design combines wild plantain seedheads with green carrot leaves, held by a small piece of crumpled wire netting in a green hock glass.

Two sprays of ash fixed on a pin-holder in a dish of water hidden by drift-wood, with a small piece of rock supporting the long swerving branch. The pots holding mauve-coloured echeveria plants are surrounded by sand.

(opposite)
The highlight of the shining pampas-grass is most effective against the greys, greens and maroon of the foliage—onopordon thistle leaves, grevillea and variegated snowberry, with one stem of dark red Berberis thunbergii.

A shallow white Brannam pottery bowl holds twisted stems of tree delphinium, fixed on a pin-holder. White tree-coral hides the holder and supports a few extra leaves.

(opposite)
A design for a modern setting uses one stem of glossy camellia foliage, held on a pin-holder in a dish of water. A piece of interesting oak root-wood hides the dish.

There are stems of several decorative leaves in this delightful arrangement in a turquoise blue vase. The outline is made with grey artemisia, and finely patterned grey centaurea flowing forward low down. A sprig of maroon-coloured rhus gives central interest, while left of centre and recessed in other places are stems of green-blue rue.

Sprays of berried berberis formed the outline of this autumn decoration, whilst corn cobs and gourds were placed for central interest. Large cabbage leaves gave a change of form and were held in crumpled wire netting.

Arrangements with
Berries, Gourds and Seedheads

Arrangements With Seedheads, Gourds and Berries

WHEN flowering time is over, rich treasures are to be found in gardens and the countryside in the form of cones, seed-pods, ferns, fungi, seedheads and berries, all of which make most interesting and permanent winter decorations.

During autumn many flat leaves, such as plane and elm, will press well between newspapers, while other coloured leaves like virginia creeper retain their colour if ironed between newspaper with a warm iron. The heat will cause the moisture to be absorbed in the paper and the ironing will keep the leaves flat.

Leaves with woody stems such as beech, rhododendron, *Magnolia grandiflora* and eucalyptus should be placed in a solution of one part glycerine and two parts water and left for three weeks. Once the solution is absorbed the leaves will turn brown and remain permanently pliable and glossy.

Seedheads of wild and garden flowers should be hung upside down until completely dry. This method allows the stems to dry straight. When collecting seedheads do not forget stems of foxgloves, acanthus, cow parsley, dock, poppy and nigella. Seed-pods of regale and other lilies as well as Japanese and Siberian iris are also useful, while grasses and corn tassles will give added attraction to most winter dry bouquets.

Gourds grow easily from seed and once they are ripe they can be varnished or painted to suit your taste.

Many winter designs can be highlighted with colourful berries and if these are brushed over with clear varnish or thin glue, they remain firm on the stems for several weeks. Place your seedheads, dried leaves, berries or gourds in the same manner that you would living plant material, reserving the bigger leaves or seedheads for low down and the finer sprays or grasses for height and outline. Apart from the collecting, which is fun and an eye opener at the same time, it is the placement of the different shapes and colours that makes these arrangements so fascinating.

Drift-wood and stones conceal the pin-holder on which are fixed five dried onion heads and some bronze green hydrangea leaves.

Sprays of beech nut pods give linear pattern to this dry design, with glycerined beech leaves and pine cones for main interest. The cones are wired at the base with hairpins and all material is held in Plasticine.

(opposite)
In this arrangement of preserved material, dried Bocconia cordata *(coral plume), teazles and poppy heads, with* Magnolia grandiflora *leaves uniting the stems low down, are held by Plasticine on a brass magazine rack.*

A decoration for a rustic setting uses berried sprays of cotoneaster and aucuba. They are fixed on a pin-holder behind a piece of wood, held firm on its base with Plasticine. Leaves low down hide the "mechanics".

(*opposite*)
A hedgerow scene built in a shallow plate. Wild dock sprays and wild arum berries and leaves are held on a pin-holder hidden by a slab of grey stone, and the design is completed with moss. Water is added.

This swerved design of leaves and yellow berries makes an elegant decoration for an autumn occasion. The foliage is weigela and Magnolia grandiflora, *held on a pin-holder in a dish of water on a shining brass kettle stand.*

Stripped ivy root gives height to this composition of brown dried dock and steel-blue echinops, all held in Plasticine on a natural-coloured wooden base. The branch is supported by stones.

A design for a country or kitchen setting of painted gourds, corn cobs, wheat and leaves, inserted in Plasticine on a wooden slab (see page 118).

Orange-coloured physalis (Cape Gooseberry), the heads cut open to reveal the berries, give central interest in this arrangement in a beige and brown pottery jar. Other dry material used are stems of brown dock, bulrushes and cream oats.

An original and beautiful wall decoration of dry material, using dock, grasses, ferns, nuts, cones and honesty. The base is a cakeboard, and the items are held in place with Copydex. The "roses" are made by inserting the honesty seedpods, first dipped in blue, into the lower scales of cones, and the nuts are "bunched" with fine wire.

(*opposite*)
Dry grasses, dock and berries make this autumn design, which is everlasting. Beige hare's tail and quaking grasses —are placed on a pin-holder in front of brown dried dock, with bronze hypericum berries inserted low down.

*A bright idea for a country setting—
decorative maize cobs with their dried leaves,
wired to a large basket lid.*

These stems of dried strawberry maize cobs need no support placed in the narrow neck of a wicker-covered wine flask.

A lichen-covered branch and sprays of berried berberis, held on a pin-holder, give height and width to another autumn design. The potato skip lid is filled with coloured gourds and ornamental sugar corn cobs.

Red candles were held by a thick ring of Plasticine to a cardboard cake stand and gave colour to this red and gold Christmas table decoration. The wheat, leaves, seedheads and cones were painted or gilded and inserted in the Plasticine.

Arrangements for Christmas

Christmas

TO celebrate means to decorate; and most of us today celebrate the festival of Christmas.

But what of decoration? I have written so many times in previous books about various methods of decorating that I must beware of repeating myself.

Most of us have used the whitewashed green branches of yew, pine and spruce. We all enjoy the red-berried holly and the glitter-flecked bowls of fruit. The shops are full of gaily coloured glass baubles and tinselled garlands, and the silver and gold painted leaves have always served us well.

The Christmas tree has been a symbol of Christmas since Victorian days and Father Christmas or Santa Claus has visited our homes to delight the children—well, ever since I can remember.

We have tried the kissing ring, the table designs, the door swags and the nativity scenes, but what is new in decorating?

I do not profess to know the full answer, even if it were needed, but in my last book PARTY PIECES I showed a number of conically shaped tree decorations, and in the following pages I present a few new ideas, which will I am sure prove useful and different to many, especially those who do not live in the country.

But it is the spirit of Christmas that counts, because it is a period set apart from the rest of the year as a time of giving and goodwill among us all. So decorate to celebrate.

To make a hanging wall or door decoration, use a cardboard cake stand as a base. Pierce a hole near the edge for the hanging cord. Then make a thick mixture of plaster powder and water, and place a mound of it at the top of the board, below the hole. Insert into this the ribbon, leaves and cones before the plaster sets. A hairpin or wire should be wound round the ribbon and cones to fix them.

(opposite)
Glittered bulrushes establish height in this gilded Christmas design for a side table. Cycas leaves give width, and cones provide central interest. All items are held by Plasticine on a gold-painted cakeboard.

A bare branch, pine and holly — but what an attractive Christmas decoration they make. The material is held on a pin-holder in a dish of water, the bright red holly berries providing central interest.

Put a ship's lantern in the window at Christmas time to welcome friends. Decorate it with ribbon and cones and sprays of pine, wired to the handle.

This Swedish-type Christmas tree is made by building up a triangle of cotton reels on to a thin slat of wood, glueing each in place. The slat is supported on a larger reel, which in turn is screwed on to a tin lid on an inverted saucer. The whole decoration is gilded, and a small coloured candle set on top.

A festive decoration in the shape of a Christmas tree, made by placing a thin layer of cottonwool between sheets of pink tissue paper and covering this with Cellophane paper. The material, clipped together with gilt paper fasteners, is cut into a half circle and folded into a cone, secured with Sellotape, and edged with tinsel ribbon. The cone is placed over a wire lampshade frame on a candlestick. Baubles and cakeboard are also gilded.

Another version of a Christmas tree, this time made from gilt wrapping paper. Cut a cone shape first, edging it with coiled cotton wool. This is stuck on with flicks of glue, as are the cosmetic cottonwool balls. Gold sequins add a touch of glitter.

A bare branch, sprays of pine and red glass baubles, fixed with ribbon into a lump of Plasticine on a slab of tree wood.

How to Do It

THE uninitiated may find it difficult to understand what goes on "behind the scenes" to hold together the items in a design and keep the material in position. How does a large piece of wood remain erect in a shallow bowl? How can fruit be prevented from rolling about in an arrangement? How is a candle fixed upright in a bowl of flowers? The photographs which follow will give you an idea of how to go about things.

Plasticine is a great boon. It will hold in place small, light pieces of wood. A thick ring of Plasticine curled round the end of a candle and pressed down on to a base will hold the candle firmly.

For an arrangement of fruit a dome of wire netting should be made to fit into the container. Small items can be held on this with toothpicks or florist's wire, or even hairpins. Large fruits like melons may be held firm on a base or tray by placing them on a curtain ring, or a rubber preserving-jar ring.

Dry leaves and stems need support because they are brittle. Make a hairpin bend with firm wire (or use a fine hairpin), place the bend at the back of the leaf and then twist one of the ends of wire round the other, at the same time encircling the stem.

Finally, these "tools" are basic necessities to the plant arranger —other items can be added as experience dictates: a pair of flower scissors, pin-holders, wire-netting (2″ mesh), Florapak or Mosette (for dry and shell arrangements), Plasticine.

One way of holding a branch of wood to a base is to press it into a lump of Plasticine.

(Below) Heavier pieces of wood should be nailed or screwed to a wooden base, which can then be stood in a container and held firmly by stones and hidden by moss or other material *(see pages 30 & 27)*.

TWO DIFFERENT WAYS OF FIXING WOOD

FIX A CANDLE
LIKE THIS . . .

When using a candle in a dry table decoration, fix a ring of Plasticine round the candle and press this down on to the container. Dry stems of oats, grasses or leaves are inserted into the Plasticine.

To make a similar arrangement with fresh plant material, surround the candle with a roll of crumpled wire netting. Fill the dish with water and insert the fresh stems into the wire, not into the Plasticine.

. . . AND DRY STEM
LIKE THIS

Plasticine is pressed on to a wooden base to hold the stems of long-eared corn which form the background to the design on p.41.

Painted leaves are inserted to hide the bare stems, and the corn cobs are set in place.

HOLD GRAPES LIKE THIS

How to use a bunch of grapes in an arrangement. Wire the end of the stalk to a false stem and (1) insert this well to the back of the container under the tallest stem so that the grapes do not appear to be drooping down from the edge of the rim (2). Add the higher placed apples on sticks (3) placing the remainder of the apples on the wire, using tooth picks if necessary to hold them in place. The finished design (not shown) was completed with large leaves at the sides.

USE A POTATO AS A HOLDER

Greenery can be inserted into a potato to make an attractive table decoration for Christmas. The potato should be flattened on one side and may need to be secured to the base by Plasticine.

How to wire a potato to make a hanging ornament.

Care of Indoor Plants

PERHAPS the best advice I can give the would-be indoor-plant arranger is not to be too ambitious at first. Many people are deterred from keeping indoor plants because they have met with one or two failures; but it is quite possible to be successful by starting off with a few easy-to-grow plants, leaving the more difficult ones until you have become practiced. Ask your florist's or nurseryman's advice about the particular needs of the plant you are buying.

Many plants in their native habitat enjoy cool shade; others like a moist, warm but not sunny atmosphere, so in general it is important to keep indoor plants away from direct sunlight, and from draughts. But although draughts are not liked, ventilation is, so do not be afraid to open the windows so that the plants can get the oxygen they need.

Avoid sudden changes of temperature—that is, a hot room in day time and cold one at night. See that the day and night temperatures do not vary more than 10° Fahrenheit.

Fork over the top soil now and again to aerate the earth, and remove all dead or yellowing leaves.

In spring and summer give your plants a fortnightly application of fertilizer, following the manufacturer's instructions. Keep the soil moist; how often to water can be learned only by experience. No fertilizer, and much less water, should be given in winter, the plant's resting time.

Be careful to water only from the bottom plants with fleshy leaves, such as African violets and *Begonia rex.* Stand them in a saucer and allow the roots to take up the food or moisture. Do not allow water to fall on the leaves. Hot water in the saucer will often give the necessary humidity needed by the plant.

As some plants like light, others shade, some heat and others cool conditions, it is better to buy a plant for a particular room, bearing in mind the spot where it will eventually stand. Most of the plants mentioned in my list are very easy to grow and most can be grouped together. If you prefer (perhaps because of colouring) a grouping of one shade-loving and another light-loving plant, arrange them together in a bowl, keeping them in their individual pots. You can remove one pot from the arrangement now and then and give it the special diet it likes for a few hours.

Picking the tips off trailing plants will make the main plant more bushy, and you can repot after three years when you think the plant is getting too big for its pot.

Plants for Decorative Grouping

Begonia rex. Provides gorgeous leaves of wine, red and silver, grey, purple and silver-green, all with a metallic sheen. The plant grows fast in summer, when it requires regular watering from the bottom. Avoid water on the leaves. Likes light, but not direct sunlight. Needs no food and very little watering in winter.

Chlorophytum. Has thin, spiky green and white striped leaves and is easy to grow and care for. Will produce baby plants at the tips of leaves which can be cut off and potted. Dislikes direct sun.

Cissus antarctica (Kangaroo vine). This plant is a tall vine-like climber and is not at all fussy. You can neglect it for weeks and it will still remain green and glossy. Never over-water. Does not mind a cool spot.

Fatshedera lizei. An attractive modern plant; grows fairly well and has leaves like very large ivy or smaller fatsia. Green or variegated. Suitable for a small room.

Fatsia japonica. Has large deep-lobed green leaves like fig leaves, which fall at all angles giving a three dimensional effect. Fast growing; likes a cool shady spot. Sponge to remove dust from leaves. Because of bare lower stems is best grouped with shorter plants.

Hedera (Ivy). These are the easiest plants for beginners to grow. They like light and do not mind a cool room. Feed once a week in spring and summer. Water sparingly in winter.

H. luzi is a light and dark green mottled variety and *H. glacier* has pale green, white-edged leaves. Good on its own or for trailing low in a group.

Maranta. There are several varieties but the kerchoveana has bright emerald green leaves with brown velvety spots and is very effective for the base of a grouping. It likes a warm, moist atmosphere. Stand the pot in a saucer of warm water occasionally.

Philodendron scandens. This is an easy climber, suitable for training up wires or on a frame. It does not need much light and prefers a cool, sunless room, yet it will stand great fluctuations of temperature and is at home on a mantelshelf over a fire or framing a doorway in the hall. If it grows too long, you can nip off a piece and insert it in a pot of leaf mould and sand, where it will easily strike again. Has green, glossy, heart-shaped leaves.

Tradescantia (Wandering Jew). In green and white, purple and green. No one should go wrong with any of the varieties. It trails and is good for wall brackets. Tips can be pinched off and will root easily in soil or water.

Asplenium nidus (Bird's-nest fern). Glossy green plant, very easy for indoor growing, giving long leathery leaves with wavy edges.

Useful Leaves For Decoration

(From Plants, Shrubs, etc.)

Acanthus. Large, shiny green pinnate leaves.

Artemisia. Several varieties. *A. ludoviciana* gives 2′ 6″ stems, of light grey foliage.

Berberis atropurpurea. Bushy in growth, giving long stems of small purple/maroon leaves.

Bergenia megasea. Large, roundish, leathery, glossy leaves.

Convolvulus concorum. Shiny, silver-grey. Tall, trailing plant.

Cytisus (Broom). Several varieties, giving long fine spikes.

Elaeagnus aureo-variegata. Shiny, golden variegated leaves.

Hosta (Funkia). Plantain Lily, several varieties, large, ribbed leaves.

Lonicera japonica aureo-reticulata. Honeysuckle-like small golden, dappled leaves; climber.

Lonicera nitida. Fine spikes of small green leaves.

Magnolia grandiflora. Large, glossy leaves, brown-felted at back.

Mahonia aquifolium. Large holly-leaved berberis. Leaves turn red in winter.

Paeonia. Leaves good after flowering has finished.

Pittosporum. Several varieties, slightly tender, small light foliage, good for outlines.

Privet. Golden or green. Good for linear effects.

Rosemary. Silver and green spikes.

Santolina (Lavender Cotton). Stems 2′ 6″, fine grey spikes.

Senecio cineraria maritima. Medium grey pinnate leaves.

Senecio greyi. Grey, white-backed leaves, smooth-edged.

Sorbus aria majestica. Whitebeam tree. Grey and pale green foliage branches.

Verbascum broussa. Large, grey-white leaves.

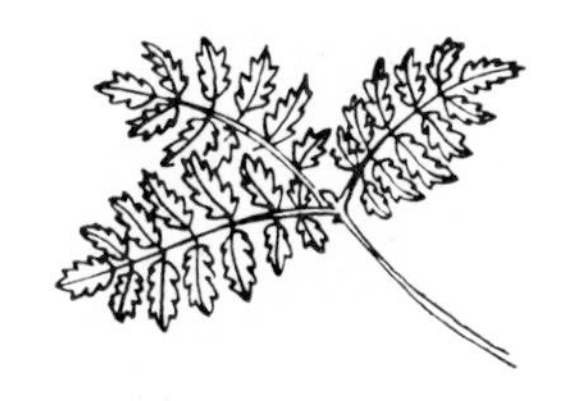

Leaves Grown From Seed

Artemisia. Grey spikes.

Coleus. Varied colours.

Canna. Maroon and green.

Castor Oil Plant. *Ricinus sanguineus*. Maroon.

Centaurea ragusina, Candissima. Grey.

Cineraria maritima, Diamond. Grey.

Cordyline indivisa. Deep green. Lanceolate (very narrow).

Euphorbia marginata. Green and white.

Fennel. Fluffy, light bottle green.

Grevillea robusta. Green.

Globe Artichoke. Grey-green, large.

Kale. Decorative, also Sutton's Glaucous. Mauve, green and purple, green and white.

Onopordum acanthium (Thistle). Grey, large, pinnate.

Perilla atropurpurea laciniata. Crimson-bronze (dull). 2′ 6″ in height.

Salvia argentea. Woolly, silvery foliage.

Smilax. Long green trails.

Verbascum (Sutton's Silver Spires). Grey, large, velvety.

Zea japonica variegata. Variegated, shiny.

Grasses

(Grasses are an ideal addition to many groupings especially dry arrangements. The following can all be grown from seed.)

Agrostis nebulosa (Cloud Grass). Superb.
Briza gracilus (Little Quaking Grass). Shakes in the breeze.
Briza maxima. Ideal when glittered at Christmas time.
Coix lachryma-jobi (Job's Tears). Curious seed pods.
Eragrostis elegans (Love Grass). Graceful.
Eulalia japonica. Long purple panicles.
Eulalia zebrina. Fine horizontal markings.
Gymnothrix latifolia. Large nodding spikes.
Hordeum jubatum (Squirreltail Grass). Like a squirrel's furry tail.
Lagurus ovatus (Hare's Tail Grass). As above, but shorter.
Miscanthus sinensis zebrinus. Hardy grass, with heads like maize, 6′ to 9′ high.
Pennisetum longistylum. Fine, rosy plumes.
Pennisetum rueppelianum. Very handsome, with abundant purple spikes.
Stipa pennata (Feather Grass).
Zea japonica quadricolor, Perfecta. Leaves streaked yellow, rose and red.
Zea japonica variegata (Variegated Maize).
Corn, Wheat and Oats are also ideal for autumn harvest decorations.

List of Suppliers

Seedsmen. For leaves, gourds, onion-heads, grasses, etc.

Bees Ltd., Corn Exchange, Liverpool 2.
Carters Tested Seeds Ltd., Raynes Park, London S.W.19.
Dobbie & Co. Ltd., Edinburgh.
Sutton & Sons, Royal Seed Establishment, Reading, Berks.
Thompson & Morgan Ltd., Ipswich, Suffolk.
W. J. Unwin Ltd., Histon, Cambs.
Edward Webb & Sons Ltd., Stourbridge, Worcs.

Plantsmen. For leaves from shrubs, trees and plants.

Hillier & Sons, West Hill Nurseries, Winchester, Hants.
Geo. Jackman & Sons Ltd., Woking Nurseries, Surrey.
R. G. Notcutt Ltd., Woodbridge, Suffolk.
L. R. Russell Ltd., Richmond Nurseries, Windlesham, Surrey.
Slieve Donard Nurseries, Newcastle, Co. Down, Eire.
Water & Son & Crisp Ltd., The Floral Mile, Twyford, Berks.

Indoor Plants.

Elm Garden Nurseries, Claygate, Surrey.
Longmans, Fenchurch Street, London E.C.
Thos. Rochford Ltd., Turnford Hall Nurseries, Broxbourne, Herts.
Wills & Segar Ltd., Brompton Road, London S.W.7.

Cacti.

Worfield Gardens, Bridgenorth, Salop.
F. M. Court, Moorland Nurseries, Stanley Park, Litherland, Lancs.

Ferns.

C. W. Grubb & Sons, Bolton-le-Sands, Carnforth, Lancs.
J. R. Taylor, Lily Hill Nurseries, Bracknell, Berks.